STOMP on SMOKING

Your Guide to Freedom from Smoking and Emotional Cravings

Break Free from Emotional Cravings and Reclaim Your Power with Self-Hypnosis

Liza Boubari

Copyright © 2025 Liza Boubari

All rights reserved. No part of this book may be reproduced or transmitted in any form or by any means, electronic or mechanical, including photocopying, recording, or by any information storage and retrieval system, without the express written permission of the publisher or author, except for the inclusion of brief quotations in a review.

The material in this book is intended for informational purposes only and is not a substitute for medical attention. By reading this, you, the reader, assume all risks for any advice given here and how you use it.

For authorized copies of this document, please contact HealWithin.com or (818) 551-1501. Enjoy reading

ISBN 978-1-7333126-9-1 (print)

ISBN 979-8-9925681-0-3 (epub)

Library of Congress Control Number: 2025902642

Second Edition

Published by HealWithin, Inc.
330 Arden Ave Suite 130
Glendale CA 91203
www.healwithin.com

Dedication

To all who struggle with the grip of smoking and the emotional cravings that bind them, may this book be your guide to freedom and empowerment.

You Matter

And to my grandmother and mother, my role models of grace, compassion, and elegance. You taught me to embrace health, nurture my body, and show kindness to others. Your unwavering wisdom inspires me to help others create lasting, positive changes.

You Matter.
With love and honor,

Liza

Table of Contents

- THE BOUBARI 3E METHOD 1
- MY STORY 2
- THE SILENT SMOKER 5
- RELAPSE AND RESILIENCE 7
- BEFORE YOU STOP SMOKING 8
- WHY HAVE YOU NOT STOPPED? 9
- FACTS ON SMOKING 11
- YOUR HEALTH 12
- BENEFITS OF SMOKING 13
- WOMEN AND SMOKING 16
- LET'S GET STARTED! 21
- IT'S TIME TO STOMP ON SMOKING 25
- WHY HYPNOSIS 26
- WHY THE BOUBARI 3E METHOD 32
- JONATHAN AND SAM'S STORY 36
- THE BOUBARI 3E METHOD 44
- STEPS TO BREAKING THE HABIT FOR GOOD 46
- 33-DAYS TO FORM NEW HABITS 48
- IT'S OKAY TO RESTART 50
- AFFIRMATIONS 51
- BONUS: SELF-HYPNOSIS PRACTICE FOR DEEPER HEALING. 52
- ABOUT LIZA 55
- TAKE THE NEXT STEP 57

THE BOUBARI 3E METHOD

You were not meant to live in limitations, whether the limitations are physical, mental, or emotional. The habit of smoking is one such limitation, and if you're reading this now, it's because something within you is ready to break through. This is no coincidence; perhaps you have been guided to this book by something greater than yourself.

Spiritual awakening is recognizing that you are connected to an energy far more powerful than any habit or behavior. By tapping into this inner power, you can rise above patterns that no longer serve you and reclaim your health, vitality, and freedom.

In the following pages, you will find the tools, techniques, and guidance to align your inner strength with your decision to quit smoking. Together, we'll walk the path of healing and transformation, reminding you with each step that you are more capable, more powerful, and more whole than you've ever imagined.

Congratulations on taking the first step toward becoming a nonsmoker.

MY STORY

So, why do I call it a journey? Because, like you, I too was once a smoker. I began smoking at the young age of 12 and continued until two years into my hypnotherapy practice. I believed that as a smoker, I could not effectively help my clients stop smoking unless I experienced the process myself. This belief became a powerful motivator, and my success in stopping solidified my conviction that change is possible.

I was a particular smoker—a smoker with rules. For instance, I never smoked in the bathroom or bedroom because I detested the lingering smell on towels and bed sheets. After a night out at a club, the first thing I would do upon returning home would be to toss my clothes into the washing machine, shower, and brush my teeth to rid myself of the cigarette odor. One day, it hit me: I had created so many rules and habits to cope with something I didn't even enjoy.

You see, we often continue repeating behaviors, expecting different results. But real change begins with a moment of clarity and a decision. My moment came when I declared, "Smoking is no longer a joy but a nuisance—I am done." Plus, I could not be smoking and helping others become nonsmokers, could I? This realization allowed me to confront the emotional connection I had to cigarettes and smoking, which turned out to be more profound and powerful than the physical act itself. I'll share more later.

Why Stomp on Smoking?

Why do I call this the Stomp on Smoking Method? Because the act of stomping on a cigarette after smoking is symbolic of conscious and deliberate behavior. Smokers often flip their cigarette stubs and stomp on them to ensure they are out and not lit. It is an act of responsibility and awareness—a good Samaritan behavior—and, interestingly, more than 90% of smokers honor this practice.

This deliberate action symbolizes the commitment and finality of its time to go or extinguish something harmful. Similarly, when you choose to stomp on smoking, you are consciously deciding to put out the habit for good. It is not just about stopping; it's about taking a decisive and intentional step toward a healthier, smoke-free life.

Congratulations on wanting to STOP Smoking

Let me applaud you for deciding to be a nonsmoker!

YES YOU CAN!

There is nothing in this world that, once you set your mind to it, you cannot accomplish. You do MATTER.

So, let's start you on healing within and living life purposefully and conscientiously. You Can Be and Live Victoriously!

For those who are not as far down the stopping process, give yourself another chance. Not everyone is wired the same way; we are all unique. Stop blaming yourself or thinking, "This is not working." You did not become a full-fledged smoker on your first try or even in the first few weeks. Success will be all up to you—plus, there is a greater reason to give yourself a chance: it will help you with a sense of self-pride and a healthier life.

Stop blaming yourself or thinking, "I have tried and it did not work." "I'm not able to quit." This is not working."

THE SILENT SMOKER

Do you know why you smoke?

Is it the comfort of a cigarette between your fingers? The way your lips curve around it? Do you feel satisfied when exhaling a cloud of smoke, imagining it as a statement of allure or defiance?

Let's dig deeper. Do you reach for a cigarette when you feel stressed, upset, irritated, angry, frustrated, or overwhelmed?

Does the first drag of nicotine make you feel loose, relaxed, and as if your problems momentarily disappear? Perhaps you believe that smoking makes you stronger, happier, or more prepared to face challenges.

Understanding these underlying emotions is crucial. Many people relapse because they have not addressed the root causes of their smoking habit. They have not learned how to handle the habitual feelings that resurface time and time again. Until these emotional triggers are confronted, stopping will feel like an uphill battle.

You did not become a full-fledged smoker on your first try or even in the first few weeks. Success will be all up to you—plus, there is a greater reason to give yourself a chance: it will help you with a sense of self-pride and a healthier life.

Overcoming the Challenges

Stopping smoking is often regarded as one of the most challenging habits to break. The withdrawal symptoms can be intense, including mood swings, irritability, depression, poor concentration, sleep disturbances, weight gain, restlessness, and even a persistent, chesty cough.

But here is the good news: these side effects are a sign that your body is healing. The discomfort is evidence that your system is recovering from the harmful effects of tobacco. It is a sign of hope.

So, how can you resist temptation and overcome the urge to light up again? There are many methods, and everyone's journey is unique. Some people choose a specific date to stop, while others wake up one morning and decide, "Today is the day." For some, the decision comes from sheer determination, while others feel compelled to stop because the suffering has become unbearable.

Regardless of your approach, preparation and support are vital. Setting a stop date and organizing both practical and emotional support can make all the difference. Understand that stopping is a process and is not to be underestimated.

RELAPSE AND RESILIENCE

Statistics show that as many as 75 percent of those who stop smoking will relapse at least once, especially those who attempt to go cold turkey. Ironically, relapses often occur weeks after overcoming the initial cravings. This is when people think, "Just one cigarette will not hurt." Before they realize it, they're back to square one.

The key is to recognize that relapsing does not mean failure. It is part of the journey. With the right tools and mindset, you can rise above the setbacks and stay committed to your goal of becoming a nonsmoker.

Remember: You are not here to quit smoking—you are here to stop smoking and become a nonsmoker. The word "quit" often carries a subconscious association with failure or giving up, but stopping is a powerful, decisive action. This book will guide you through the process, helping you understand the deeper connections to your smoking habit and providing practical tools to break free.

Let's embark on this journey together.

BEFORE YOU STOP SMOKING

Choosing the Stomp on Smoking Method

Let's just say today is the day you choose to stomp on smoking and become healthier.

If you opt for nicotine replacement support, I want you to be reminded that it is only a temporary answer. Yet many people feel that such an improvement in their health motivates them to become nonsmokers. Kudos to you!

My client Sam agrees: "It was hard at first, and I did get cravings." Five months in, he stated: "I feel fitter, I enjoy running more, I can push further in the gym, and I somehow concentrate better. Food has more oomph to it, too. There is no going back now."

Is your Stop Smoking Date set?   YES?

What is the date? _____

If you are interested in learning more about one-on-one sessions to Stomp on Smoking, please call us for a free, no-obligation consultation to become a vibrant and healthy nonsmoker.

YOU CAN!

WHY HAVE YOU NOT STOPPED?

Most smokers want to stop smoking for many reasons: health, social stigma, and feeling like a slave to their smoking habit. So why do they find it challenging to stop? The problem lies in the disconnect between the conscious and subconscious minds.

The Conscious Mind

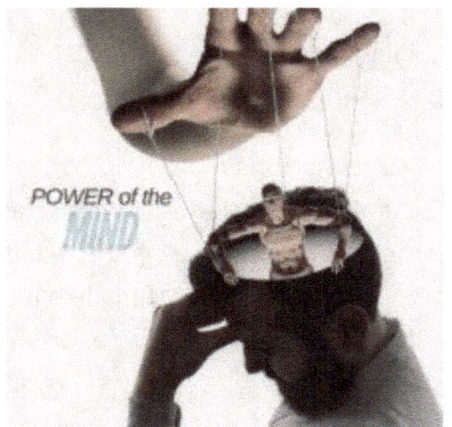

The conscious mind wants to stop. This is the part of your mind that reads the research, health reports, and news about how harmful smoking is to your health. It is known that smoking is now banned in all public places and that fewer and fewer people see smoking as glamorous or cool. Instead, it's viewed as a bad habit. The conscious mind also understands that smoking is expensive, smells bad, and the list goes on.

The conscious mind says:

- It's bad for me.
- It smells.
- It's expensive.
- It's not acceptable.
- It's out of line with who I am.

The Subconscious Mind

However, the subconscious mind, the larger and more powerful part of the brain, doesn't understand any of these logical, rational reasons. Instead, it operates based on ingrained habits and emotional associations. The subconscious mind says:

- It helps me survive.
- I can't stop.
- It's my friend.
- I'll gain weight.
- It helps me relax.

The subconscious mind holds onto smoking as a comfort mechanism, associating it with relaxation, breaks, or enjoyable moments like having a cigarette with coffee or after intimacy. Some say - "there is nothing like a cigarette and a glass of wine" or "I have to smoke when I'm driving!"

FACTS ON SMOKING

Did you know?

- Among young teens (aged 13 to 15), about one in five smoke worldwide, and one in four teens pick up smoking.

- Between 80,000 and 100,000 children worldwide start smoking every day—roughly half of whom live in Asia.

- Evidence shows that around 50% of those who start smoking in adolescent years go on to smoke for 15 to 20 years.

- Peer-reviewed studies show teenagers are heavily influenced by tobacco advertising.

Cigarettes: Stimulants, Not Relaxants

Here is something most people do not realize: cigarettes are stimulants, not relaxants. When you smoke, your blood sugar and heartbeat rise, and your heart palpitates faster. Smoking does not physically relax you. The sense of relaxation comes solely from your mind, which tells your body, "Ahhhhh, I now feel relaxed and in control." This perceived relaxation is a mental trick, perpetuating the habit.

YOUR HEALTH

Half of long-term smokers will die from tobacco. Every cigarette smoked cuts at least five minutes of life on average—about the time taken to smoke it.

Smoking is the single largest preventable cause of disease and premature death. It is a prime factor in heart disease, stroke, and chronic lung disease. It can cause cancer of the lungs, larynx, esophagus, mouth, and bladder, and contributes to cancer of the cervix, pancreas, and kidneys.

Lung cancer is the deadliest form of cancer, killing more people than breast, colon, and prostate cancer combined.

More than 4,000 toxic or carcinogenic chemicals have been found in tobacco smoke.

One British survey found that nearly 99% of women did not know of the link between smoking and cervical cancer.

At least a quarter of all deaths from heart disease and about three-quarters of the world's chronic bronchitis sufferers are related to smoking. Smoking-related diseases cost the United States more than $240 billion a year.

BENEFITS OF SMOKING

Anything that you think is a benefit of smoking is a mental choice and an emotional benefit. There are no real physical benefits to smoking.

There are many, many reasons to stop smoking. Here are a few good reasons to stop:

- Short and Long-Term Benefits
- Social Benefits
- Specific Benefits to Women
- Specific Benefits to Seniors
- Life Expectancy

Short and Long-Term Benefits

20 minutes after the last cigarette

- Blood pressure and pulse rate drop to normal.
- Hand and foot temperature rises to normal.

8 hours after the last cigarette

- Blood carbon monoxide levels drop to normal.
- Blood oxygen level increases to normal.

1 day after the last cigarette

- Chances of heart attack and stroke start decreasing.

2 days after the last cigarette

- Sense of taste and smell begin to heighten.
- Certain nerve endings begin to re-grow.
- Nicotine by-products are removed from the body.

3 days after the last cigarette

- Bronchial tubes start to relax, making breathing easier.
- Lung capacity begins to improve.

2 to 12 weeks after the last cigarette

- Walking and aerobic exercises become easier.

There are many, many reasons to stop smoking. Here are a few good reasons to stop:

- Short and Long-Term Benefits
- Social Benefits
- Specific Benefits to Women
- Specific Benefits to Seniors
- Life Expectancy
- Walking and aerobic exercises become easier.

2 years after the last cigarette

- The risk of recurrence of ulcers is reduced.
- The ability for short-term healing is improved.
- The risk of death from heart disease declines by 24%.

3 to 5 years after the last cigarette

- The risk of heart attack and stroke approaches that of someone who has never smoked.
- The risk of developing mouth, esophageal, throat, and bladder cancer is reduced by 50%.

5-10 years after the last cigarette

- Pre-cancerous cells are replaced by healthy, normal cells.
- There is a 50% to 70% reduction in the risk of developing lung cancer.
- The risk of pancreatic cancer is reduced.
- The risk of developing Heart Disease drops to that of someone who never smoked.

Social Benefits

- If you pay any health insurance, your premiums will decrease.
- You'll feel in control instead of feeling that cigarettes control you.
- You'll feel an enhanced sense of self-esteem.
- Your family will no longer be subjected to second-hand smoke, and as a result, they'll be healthier now and in the future.
- You'll begin to gain a healthy appearance.
- You won't have to leave any non-smoking gatherings just to smoke.
- Smoking is very expensive – you'll see your bank account grow, or you can put your money towards something that you've always wanted.
- Compared to smokers, people who stop are more likely to exercise regularly.

WOMEN AND SMOKING

Women who smoke often face a complex relationship with their habit—one rooted in emotional, social, or even cultural triggers. Often providing a temporary sense of calm, a perceived escape from stress, or a way to connect in social settings. Yet, the pull of nicotine and the ritual of smoking can mask deeper emotional cravings or unresolved feelings.

While smoking may feel like a source of control or comfort, it ultimately takes a toll on physical health, self-esteem, and overall well-being. For many, breaking free from smoking is not just about quitting a habit—it's about reclaiming their power, health, and inner peace.

You know, if you're pregnant or planning to get pregnant, this is such a pivotal moment in your life—one filled with love, hope, and so many dreams for your baby. But if smoking is still a part of your life, it's worth considering how it could affect not just you, but that tiny life growing inside you. Nicotine and the chemicals from cigarettes don't just stay in your body; they're transferred through your bloodstream to your baby, where it may impact their development in ways you'd never guess.

Even beyond that, the smell and residue from smoking stay on your lips, your fingers, and your skin. So, when you hold or kiss your baby, you're unknowingly transferring those toxins to their fragile skin. And it's not just about you—if your partner smokes, the same thing happens.

Skin-to-skin contact, which should be the most nurturing, loving connection, can unintentionally expose your baby to harmful chemicals. Not only that, but the smell of smoke becomes embedded in your baby's subconscious. For some, this could create a subconscious association that smoking is normal or acceptable. Others may have the opposite effect, registering as an awful, repulsive smell. Either way, your baby's body might unknowingly respond by feeling uneasy or even repelled by those who hold them, disrupting the bond you're working so hard to create.

Breaking free from smoking is more than just a health choice—it's about giving your baby the purest start in life, free from unnecessary risks and subconscious confusion. You have the power to make that happen, for both of you.

Stopping smoking during pregnancy is one of the best decisions you can make—for your baby and yourself. And I know it's not just about stopping; it's about staying smoke-free after your baby is born. Many women quit during pregnancy but pick it back up later, often because of stress or old habits. But this time, you can choose a different path—one that prioritizes your health, your baby's health, and your future. You have the strength to make this change, and there's help and support available to guide you every step of the way. You've got this.

- If women didn't smoke during pregnancy, fetal and infant deaths would be reduced by approximately 10%.
- Women who stop smoking before pregnancy or during the first 3 to 4 months of pregnancy have the same low risk of having a low-birth-weight baby as women who have never smoked.
- For women who stop smoking in the later stages of pregnancy, infants have higher birth weight compared to women who continue to smoke.
- Two years after the last cigarette, their risk of cervical cancer is reduced.
- Nonsmokers reach menopause 1 - 2 years later than smokers.

Let's figure out the cost for your health.

Today, most cigarettes cost about $11 a pack. If you are a regular smoker, then on average, you smoke about 10 cigarettes a day, a pack can last two days.

$11/2 = $5.50 per day
$5.50 x 7 = $38.50 per week
$38.50 x 4 = $154.00 per month
$154.00 x 12 = $1,848.00 per year.

If you smoke one pack a day, then double the prices you paid and help destroy your gums, tongue, face/skin, throat, lungs, blood circulation, and so on. Do you have any idea what you or a student can do with $3,696.00 a year in a bank account? Could you use half of it to take a relaxing or dream trip somewhere?

Before You Stop Smoking, know some facts.

Cigarette smoke contains over 4,000 chemicals, including 43 known cancer-causing (carcinogenic) compounds. These include nicotine, tar, carbon monoxide, formaldehyde, ammonia, hydrogen cyanide, arsenic, and DDT.

Cigarette flavors have changed many times since they were first made. Initially, cigarettes were unfiltered, allowing the full "flavor" of the tar to come through. As the public became concerned about the health effects of smoking, filters were added to remove the bitter taste. However, filters do not make cigarettes safer.

The solution to the bitter-tasting cigarette was easy ---*Feel the sweetness* - the *brownish moistness*? Common additives to help cigarettes taste better include **yeast, wine, caffeine, beeswax, sweetener, and chocolate**. As the tobacco industry's saying goes... "*An addicted customer is a customer for life, no matter how short that life is.*"

Make sure that YOU have the last laugh.

Stopping any habit such as smoking - is always YOUR option. Only YOU have full control over what goes in your mouth and your body.

Leading Causes of Death in US	Percentage of Total Number	Number of Deaths
Smoking tobacco	20%	480,000
Preventable medical errors	10%	210-250,000
Being overweight and obese	9%	280-300,000

Leading Causes of Death in CA	Deaths	Rate	State Rank	U.S. Rate
1. Heart Disease	165.0	62,797	142.9	40th
2. Cancer	152.5	59,516	136.7	45th
3. Stroke	37.6	16,355	37.6	24th
4. Alzheimer's Disease	31.0	16,238	37.1	14th
5. Chronic Respiratory	40.9	13,881	32.2	44th
6. Accidents	49.4	13,840	33.1	50th
7. Diabetes	21.5	9,595	22.1	20th (tie)
8. Influenza/Pneumonia	14.3	6,340	14.6	23rd (tie)

Figures are based on the most recent CDC data available, but may vary slightly from year to year

LET'S GET STARTED!

Take time to answer each question.

Have you ever sat down to list your reasons for wanting to stop smoking?   Yes____ No____

Is it for you and your family's health? Is it to save money or to prevent wrinkles? Or, is it because of what the doctors told you, the harsh cough, asthma, or have you just had enough?

Take a few moments to answer these simple questions.

Do you remember when you started smoking?

___

Did someone give it to you? Did you pick it up from someone or somewhere?

___

Who in your childhood smoked?

___

Was it normal to have smoking in your household?

___

Did you pick it up because you were bullied or wanted to fit in (peer pressure)?

_____

What are your rituals for smoking?
(i.e., with coffee, after dinner, in the car...)

_____

How will you deal with stress or anger?
(keeping your hands or mouth busy).

_____

Find an activity for when the urge to smoke hits.
(Urges are not long-lasting. Breathe, drink water, chew gum.

_____

List your reason(s) for wanting to stop smoking.
(For your and your family's health, save money, prevent wrinkles, or the doctor told you so).

_____

Everyone stops differently.

What best describes your pattern of smoking?

1. I have at least 10 cigarettes a day   _____
2. I only smoke after work   _____
3. I only smoke occasionally   _____

When was your last cigarette?

4. Less than an hour ago   _____
5. More than 4 hours ago   _____
6. More than 24 hours ago   _____

How many cigarettes do you smoke?

_____

How many years have you smoked?

_____

How soon after you wake up do you have your first cigarette?

Within 5 minutes   _____
10-30 minutes   _____
30-60 minutes   _____

How many times have you tried to quit and lasted not more than 24 hours?

_____

Have you made attempts at quitting before? (If yes)

Do you remember what caused you to start smoking again?

_____

As a nonsmoker, how do you imagine your life to be better or different?

___

Have you ever quit and felt a sense of withdrawal?
(If yes) describe the feeling(s):

___

Are you ready to get off this vicious cycle, the treadmill, the slavery to smoking and tobacco?

___

How many other smokers do you live with?

___

Are you ready to reclaim your health and your rights and become healthier?

___

If you said YES ... You CAN be a nonsmoker!
Be ready to **Live Victoriously** - in the moment.
Be open to breathing oxygen and vitality.
Be willing to learn **Self-hypnosis**.

IT'S TIME TO STOMP ON SMOKING

Most smokers have experienced it more than once. Several weeks down the road to quitting for good, then... **One button gets pushed, one slip, one puff, and all that effort goes to waste.**

Here is why: Because addiction is very clever, that's why, and it works at an unconscious level. So, however strong your conviction is to start with, addiction waits until you are at a low point and then strikes. And suddenly, you find yourself making up the most incredibly creative reasons for why it's OK to have 'just - that one.'

We highly recommend:

1- Listen to the *Stomp on Smoking* audio recording for 33 consecutive days.

2- Wear the bracelet and repeat your daily affirmations while turning each bead. This process will anchor your promise to yourself — I Matter

WHY HYPNOSIS

Wikipedia:

Hypnosis is a human condition involving focused attention, reduced peripheral awareness, and an enhanced capacity to respond to suggestions.

What does hypnosis feel like?

I usually get a certain look when people find out that I am a clinical hypnotherapist. They often begin with "Don't look me in the eye" or "Can you hypnotize me now?" leading to "Can you help me quit smoking?" or "What is it like?" For the last question, I think they mean, "What does it feel like?"

Hypnosis feels different to different people. Some people go deeper and seem able to relax to a deeper level, while others may only go into a light trance or relaxation. Usually, the more hypnosis you have experienced, the faster and more you can go into a deeper level of trance state. It is a skill to be able to allow your mind to go to a deeper level of trance. The best way to describe what hypnosis feels like is to talk about what one of my clients experienced in his session with me.

Client's Experience

I remember quite clearly the first time I was hypnotized. I was referred to Liza for panic and anxiety, plus I was told I had to lose over 20 lbs. I had wondered what hypnosis was like for many years, and I must admit, curiosity if she could help me lose weight and overcome my panic was a huge factor in coming to see her.

Sitting in her recliner, she asked me to stare at a spot and close my eyes only when I was ready. Inwardly, I was thinking, "I don't know her, and I'm surrendering all my control in a place I have never been to before." However, I quickly got over this feeling and reasoned I trusted her.

I closed my eyes and could feel my heart beating quicker. Paranoid thoughts started to enter my mind. I had never seen a demonstration of hypnotherapy before. The only hypnosis I had witnessed was stage hypnosis, and that was as an observer, not a subject. What if she were to make me do or say something embarrassing to demonstrate the magical powers of hypnosis? I opened my eyes slightly and slyly peeped around. She smiled!

I allowed my eyes to close once more and began listening to her words. Liza talked in a slow, comforting voice, softly whispering at times. At first, Liza asked me to focus on my breathing, directing me to take slow, deep breaths. This immediately began to calm me down. My heart began to slow, and I felt comfortably relaxed.

She gave suggestions for becoming aware of my body, walking down steps, and feeling more deeply relaxed with each downward step. Every time she said the words 'deeper relax,' I felt a wave of relaxation surge from my brain and flow through my whole body. This is all right, I thought.

Soon, I began thinking to myself, "I can still hear her. I still know who I am and where I am...Is this it?" I felt pleasantly comfortable and relaxed but was a little disappointed that nothing 'magical' was happening. After taking stock of my thoughts for a few moments, I reasoned that I did not want anything 'magical' to happen to me. I realized that I should be content and go with the flow.

However, my mind quickly countered, "Maybe something magical IS happening to me. How do I know that I can move my hand? How do I know if I do have control? What if this control is just an illusion?" I thought to myself, "Shall I try and move my hand? Yes, let's see what happens." I delicately twitched the fingers in my left hand just a little. My arm was so heavy, I could not lift my arm, yet my fingers still worked! I can move!

No one was 'in control' of me. This shattered my perception of hypnosis, but at the same time comforted me. "This feels like meditation." I could stand up and walk out of the room any time I chose – just as Liza said. All this hype about hypnosis- then the strangest thing happened.

I could hear Liza counting, "Five, four, three, two, one, and fully wide awake," as my mind seemed to be lifted back to reality. With my blinking eyes, I scanned around her office with a glazed expression. I noticed my hands felt numb and a little cold.

After a few seconds, I managed to re-orient myself back to reality, and I looked at the clock. Fifty minutes had passed, but it only seemed like 5 – weird! I felt somehow calmer and more relaxed than I probably had ever felt in my whole life. Nothing weird or 'magical' had happened, but it worked; I felt calm and relaxed. I felt great!

Why Hypnosis Works

Through hypnosis (guided visualization and powerful positive suggestions), we use every single psychological trick that smoking addiction plays on you to free you from its grip. Our hypnosis sessions will gently move your mind from its current habitual state to complete freedom from cigarettes to feeling good! No longer will you be controlled by the need to smoke.

No more planning your day so you can smoke, no more running outside at work or gatherings, worrying whether you have enough cigarettes left. No more spraying perfume to change the stink. No more lying to your loved ones.

You can use hypnosis to:

1. improve memory, concentration, and study habits.
2. change habits such as smoking, overeating, or nail-biting
3. control urges and weight
4. boost self-esteem and confidence
5. improve sleep patterns and athletic abilities
6. reduce stress and anxiety
7. overcome fears and phobias, speaking in public, etc.
8. reduce pain
9. create better habits – creating healthier choices and patterns in mind and body.

Now – Let's Take Action:

The best way to honor your decision and commitment to YOU is to remove all reminders of smoking from your surroundings – such as ashtrays, the emergency stash or pack, and even one cigarette hidden somewhere. Do your best to stay away from places that may be a trigger – at least for 3 days.

One of the main reasons we find why it's EASIER and not traumatic or difficult to stop smoking with our unique hypnosis method is that the nature of the technique lets us take the pleasure associated with smoking and transfer it to a healthier habit of the smoker's choice (e.g., relaxing, exercising, drinking water, etc.).

Therefore, with Stomp on Smoking and HealWithin's techniques, the chance of you gaining weight or other undesirable side effects associated with stopping smoking is minimal. The only "side effects" are benefits that you receive when you become a nonsmoker - an increase in vitality and health, relief from the sneaking around, freedom, and peace of mind!

> The US Food and Drug Administration has a list of approved smoking cessation products. Electronic cigarettes are not FDA-approved for smoking cessation and could be more harmful than tobacco products. Substances found in e-cigarette aerosol can pose a risk for decreased lung development, breathing difficulties, lower defense against bacterial and viral pathogens, and vaping-induced inflammatory reactions that can mimic metastatic cancer. They have the potential to go deep into the lungs and may pose a risk for diseases not usually seen in smokers. Some prescribed smoking cessation drugs have been associated with behavior changes, agitation and hostility, and depression or an increase in its symptoms. Talk to your doctor right away if you notice any of these symptoms.

Smokers are encouraged to wean themselves off any tobacco products after they have broken the social habits associated with smoking. Heavier or longer-term smokers may need extra help. Smoking cessation drugs can be prescribed and have been proven to be successful.

A study from the University of California in Los Angeles found that nicotine replacements alter the way the brain responds to smoking cues, making it easier to resist cravings.

WHY THE BOUBARI 3E METHOD

Why the Boubari 3E Method STOMP ON SMOKING method makes becoming a nonsmoker easier...

Here is why. As you learn to go into a hypnotic state (trance), you will feel relaxed, begin to breathe easier, and be free of that old smoking habit, not feeling stressed, not feeling like you made a sacrifice or are missing out. Most importantly, the urge to smoke will subside.

Hypnosis isn't magic but a powerful, relaxing state that almost everyone can access. You must be willing. Once the mind is in the state of hypnosis, the unconscious mind (which is usually resistant to change in our normal waking state) becomes more open to ideas of change. When the person being hypnotized consciously wants the change, suggestions are given that the unconscious can accept, so that both the conscious and unconscious mind can be aligned to make the powerful decision to become a nonsmoker.

What you will feel is a huge sense of pride and relief that you have finally accomplished what all smokers long to achieve: becoming a happy, healthy, and permanent nonsmoker.

Usually, when a smoker "tries" to stop either on their own or with other methods, they feel miserable and suffer the depression brought on by feeling that "something's missing" and that they are being deprived of their escape, pleasure, or crutch.

The brilliance of hypnosis and the HealWithin Stomp on Smoking specialized treatment, in particular, is that it takes away the feeling of being deprived. It removes dependency and the need to smoke. Even the need for outside aids, gimmicks, or replacements becomes unnecessary.

No e-cigarettes, patches, or nicotine gum. No herbal remedies, acupuncture, or lasers. Hypnosis is as painless as sitting back in a pleasant, comfortable chair and relaxing…nice and easy!

We offer discounted follow-up sessions at HealWithin with anchoring sessions for three consecutive months after your initial stop-smoking session.

Forty percent of smokers fail within the initial three-month period. Plan a regular, healthful reward for being a nonsmoker. Take the money you save by not buying cigarettes and spend it on yourself or a loved one. It's not about the money, but you being proud of yourself!

Are you with me?   Do you relate? Are you smiling yet?

Yep – how many of those times have you had?

You smoke when happy or sad, angry or calm, celebrating or feeling blue.

These are all EMOTIONS you feel. Just as you come to feel them, you light a cigarette and shut down the feeling that was about to rise and come to the surface. What you do not realize is how often you have suppressed your feelings.

Time to embrace your feelings.

I explain to each of my stop-smoking clients, or when I speak to a group, that what you do is you knowingly and unknowingly suppress what you want to communicate: voice, even thoughts, and feelings, truly. Often without realizing or knowing, cigarettes become your silent buddy system, always there for you.... You just reach out, and there it is. Of course, bear in mind, "IT" is not there – you went and purchased it, unpacked it, lit it, and placed it in between your lips to feel better – because IT helps you feel good, and THAT is the feeling You LIKE – not the rolled-up paper with all the nicotine and embalming solutions and all other pollutants in it. It's not about cigarettes, but what emphasis and feelings you attach to that rolled-up paper.

In a way, it's really simple and silly – isn't it? Is this making sense yet? Does this make it easier for you to let IT go?

IT is NOT your friend. If you had a friend who stole from you, no matter how pretty or handsome, hurt or belittled you, would you still want that friend to be part of you? Let alone hold it, caress it, and give it so much power over you?

If you're going to quit smoking, do the job right.

There are a million and one ways to stop smoking... from nicotine patches and chewing gum to tablets, lozenges, inhalers, and Chantix – Zyban is supposed to help with withdrawal symptoms. In addition, plenty of people are willing to tell you how to stop smoking - quitting tips are everywhere. But they all miss one vital component - the unconscious mind.

The human body is a fantastic instrument because it protects and shields itself for survival. During sleep, the body's immune system helps a smoker eliminate some of the nicotine poison, thus venting the buildup of lethal doses. This explains why you have not died instantly or in just a few months. Nicotine poisoning does its damage over time and travels throughout the body.

JONATHAN AND SAM'S STORY

Jonathan's Story

When Jonathan's father developed throat cancer after never smoking at all, Jonathan, who had smoked since he was 15, decided to stop at the age of 32.

Jonathan said, "I felt guilty that I smoked and was considered healthy, not realizing I was doing so poorly. I did cut back to one or two smokes a day. Unfortunately, the pressures of daily life, stress at work, the brink of a divorce, dealing with doctors, and child custody got to me until I was back to smoking 10-12 cigarettes a day, and one pack on nights out. It helped me deal with the pressures. But today, I feel I can handle situations without a cigarette thanks to you, Liza."

Sam's Story

Sam's girlfriend Angela is not happy with Sam's smoking and begins nagging him to stop. Sam announced that he would quit on his coming birthday and called HealWithin.

After the first session, he went home and had a good night's sleep. In his second session, he confessed to smoking not because he enjoyed it but out of habit. On his third session, he walked in smiling because he had not had a single cigarette the whole week. Not only had Angela stopped nagging, but she also started walking with him. In less than four sessions, not only did Sam stop smoking, but they both felt better!

Smoking or Not, It Is a Choice

Whatever method you choose, choosing the right modality doubles your chances of success. We all need to find a powerful personal reason to stop smoking, as that will help us sustain momentum. Most people don't choose to save money to drive their behavior change. It is more likely to be personal: for children, your wife or husband, or because the doctor informs you of pregnancy or some form of threat to your health.

When clients want to book a stop-smoking session with me, I ask why they want to stop and why now.

> **Remember - it takes 3 minutes for urges to go away. No matter what your urges, busy yourself for three minutes, and the initial urge fades away.**

Simple, practical ideas can help, too:

I ask my clients to keep a simple diary (notepad) to keep tabs on the triggers that make them want a cigarette. Jot down something to just become aware of how many, when, and why.

I also ask them, right before they have a smoke, to hold the cigarette in their hand and question themselves: "Do I want this, or do I need this?" Most often, it is a want, not a need. Your body does not need it – you think it does. You can begin TODAY by doing these two exercises to discover your thoughts and feelings.

Think about when you enjoy a cigarette and when you need one, then anticipate how you will cope in such circumstances. For instance:

- If you always have a cigarette with coffee, cut out the coffee. Have tea, fruit juice, or water instead. Switch the association with was.
- If you feel the urge to eat instead of smoking, opt for a sensible alternative such as gum, fruit, or a Popsicle.
- If you regularly go out for a drink and associate drinking with cigarettes, avoid the bar scene for a few days.

- If your friends are smokers and keep going outside to smoke, it might be tempting to join them. Busy yourself with something else and know that you do not have to join in. By doing so, you may just become a source of inspiration to them.

Identify distractions that can replace the desire to smoke:

1. Physical exercise, chatting with a friend, or drinking water can help a lot. Remember one thing: Cravings increase in intensity for up to three minutes and then subside.

2. Plan how you will distract yourself for three to five minutes at a time. For example:
   - Practice deep breathing.
   - Validate how your fingers and skin smell so much fresher.
   - Acknowledge that you cough less and feel a sense of accomplishment.
   - Above all, stay on course.

You tried, and it did not work.

Many say, "I tried many times, and it does not work." You tried it and began eating more and even gained weight, and by golly, that is not acceptable. You may have become more irritated, anxious, or even angry.

Overheard: "You know, lady, you don't smoke. The cigarette does all the smoking, you are just the sucker!"

Free Yourself of Smoking and Guilt

There is a profound difference between a smoker who has stopped smoking and a nonsmoker. The smoker resists cigarettes, while the nonsmoker cannot imagine anything worse than smoking. Which would you rather be?

Your decision to stop ingesting nicotine is a choice to live longer and healthier. You are trading smoking for a life filled with vitality, cleanliness, and happiness.

Remember, you are not "trying" ...
The Key is not to "try' – just do. Once you know and are capable of doing something, then "Trying" to quit only tells your subconscious mind, "I'm trying–not choosing." Not buying any but bumming cigarettes from others is again the same message – telling your inner-self that a little cheating is OK.

A conscious determination to stop smoking builds inner conflict. One part of your mind wants to quit and says,

"I am ready to quit smoking". The other sees the negative and says, "No way, it's too hard, I can't do this." It's as if opposing forces within you are fighting for supremacy. With the first emotional moment of pressure or excitement, the older, stronger pattern conquers the new, younger one, backing you into the old habits.

Not everyone who stops smoking gains weight or gets angry. But if you gain more than a few pounds, I can also help you through this. And remember, smoking is an oral gratification – so is eating.

Understand the Need

Psychological Need – Powerful Emotions

Smoking often becomes a reward system for many people. You reward yourself with a cigarette after doing something good. When something goes wrong, you avoid feelings by smoking. When blocked creatively, you pace and puff, hoping for a breakthrough. It's as if the cigarette is your muse.

In reality, a piece of paper filled with tobacco is neither a tranquilizer, a security blanket, nor a reward. But you made it so. It is only real in your mind. You associate smoking with these feelings and are programmed to link the effects of smoking with gratification. Simple and silly, isn't it?

What Are You Stuffing Instead of Expressing?

Repressed feelings are often cited as reasons for smoking. You may have forgotten how to express true feelings of anger, hurt, or disagreement. Instead of expressing these emotions, you smoke to alleviate emotional turmoil. Smoking may even mask feelings of resentment, conflict, or self-loathing, especially if you feel like a failure for not stopping.

One client started smoking in her early thirties after losing her aunt, who had raised her. Picking up a cigarette from her aunt's dresser gave her a sense of closeness. She continued smoking for 28 years until she came to me. Through hypnosis, she realized she didn't need cigarettes to keep her aunt's memory alive. She let go of the habit and embraced the loving memories instead.

Free Yourself of Smoking and Guilt

There is a profound difference between a smoker who has stopped smoking and a nonsmoker. The smoker resists cigarettes, while the nonsmoker cannot imagine anything worse than smoking. Which would you rather be?

Your decision to stop ingesting nicotine is a choice to live longer and healthier. You are trading smoking for a life filled with vitality, cleanliness, and happiness.

Remember, you are not "trying" to stop — you are deciding to become a nonsmoker. The choice is yours, and it's a trade entirely in your favor!

Just so you know - when you STOP smoking, you <u>are not giving up pleasure</u>. You are giving up the poison, guilt, shame, hurt, and, yes, nicotine. It's that simple.

Say YES to YOU! You Matter

Reasons People Don't Stop the Smoking Habit

So why do you keep smoking despite knowing all this? The answer is simple: inner FEAR.

- Fear of giving up your perceived pleasure, crutch, or "friend."
- Fear of feeling anxious, stressed, or angry.
- Fear of gaining weight, either from eating more or slowing metabolism.
- Fear that withdrawal will be too traumatic.
- Fear of losing regular bowel movements.
- Fear of giving up a life's pleasure.
- Fear that cravings will never go away, even after stopping.
- Fear that quitting won't stick.
- Fear of being afraid itself.
- Fear of failure because others couldn't stop.

All these smaller fears stem from one big fear: THE FEAR that stopping smoking will be too difficult and painful—and that you might fail. No one wants to feel like a failure.

THE BOUBARI 3E METHOD

As humans, we are conditioned from a young age to believe, "You never quit," and "You are no quitter." So, when it comes to stopping smoking, it's not about quitting, it's about making a choice. The choice to stop smoking is yours, just as the choice to start once was. This decision must come from within, not because someone else says so.

Explore Why to Choose HealWithin and the Stomp on Smoking Method

1. **Embrace Who You Are:** Accepting yourself fully can be the most liberating moment of your life. Recognize that "just one" cigarette is too many, and thousands will never be enough.

2. **End the Games:** Nicotine dependency recovery is all or nothing. Follow one rule to ensure success: No nicotine today!

3. **Measure Victory:** Forget the overwhelming idea of quitting "forever." Instead, focus on staying a nonsmoker one day at a time. Celebrate small victories—hour by hour, day by day, week by week, or set a goal like 33 consecutive days.

4. **Navigate Emotional Recovery:** For some, nicotine dependency has been a deeply ingrained relationship, influencing almost every aspect of their life. Be prepared to experience an emotional journey through phases such as

denial, anger, bargaining, depression, acceptance, and complacency. Understanding this process can help you heal.

5. **Do Not Skip Meals:** Nicotine acts as a stimulant, masking symptoms like hunger or low blood sugar. When stopping, eat regularly and avoid hunger-related symptoms like irritability or difficulty concentrating. Drink acidic fruit juice, like cranberry juice, during the first three days to help remove nicotine from your system, then switch to water.

6. **Avoid Crutches:** A crutch—whether a person, product, or activity—creates reliance that may increase relapse risk if removed. Instead, lean on a supportive, experienced nonsmoker or ex-smoker for guidance and motivation.

7. **Craving Coping Techniques:** Cravings are short but intense. Recognize the triggers and plan distractions such as physical exercise, chatting with a friend, or drinking water. Cravings usually subside within three minutes, so focus on staying calm and redirecting your energy during this brief period.

STEPS TO BREAKING THE HABIT FOR GOOD

1. Assess the Habit: Identify the bad habit you want to change and when or where it is most likely to occur. For example, if you're trying to stop smoking, your list might include:
   - With coffee
   - In the car on the way to work
   - During an afternoon break with a coworker
2. Avoid Triggers: Once you've identified the links to your behavior, find ways to avoid them. For example:
   - Spend breaks in a nonsmoking area or with a coworker who doesn't smoke.
   - Share your goals with friends and ask for their support in choosing smoke-free locations.
   - Replace routines—instead of sitting on the porch after dinner, go for a walk.
3. Replace the Habit: Build a new habit to replace the one you're trying to stop. Every time you feel the urge to smoke:
   - Chew gum to keep your mouth occupied.
   - Take a moment to reconnect with your reasons for stopping.
   - Choose healthy distractions, such as physical activity or deep breathing.

Habits are formed through neural pathways, and exposure to familiar cues can cause a relapse. If this happens, be gentle with yourself—every attempt helps forge new pathways.

Hourly Breathing Exercise: Every hour, pause and take three deep breaths. Hold for a moment, then exhale, releasing all stress and tension. Notice how good it feels! Every day before going to bed and as you wake up, you repeat this affirmation: **TODAY, I AM A NONSMOKER**

You Have the Power

Remember: **You have always had the power within you to change.** Every step you take toward breaking free from smoking is a victory for your health, happiness, and well-being. You've decided to stop smoking—now commit to it, embrace it, and celebrate the incredible, healthier version of yourself.

33-DAYS TO FORM NEW HABITS

Liza's 33-Day Theory on Forming New Habits

You may have heard the phrase, "It takes 21 days to form a habit." My philosophy is that it takes **33 consecutive days** to change and form a new habit.

Why 33 instead of 21 days? We are creatures of habit, and our lives are structured by time: seconds, minutes, hours, days, weeks, and months. The longest month is 31 days. By continuing a new routine for 33 days, you surpass the full month and start the next. This instills confidence to continue: "If I can do it for over a month, I can do it for another."

This approach eliminates the pressure of "possible failure" and builds momentum. By the second month, the new habit is ingrained, and success reinforces itself. Success feeds success, and the "it" you conquer is YOU. If this method doesn't work, hypnosis can address deeper subconscious blocks.

Be The Success You Wish to See!

Know what to expect: Physical withdrawal symptoms typically last one to three weeks. After that, it's all psychological.

- Do activities incompatible with smoking, such as bicycling, jogging, hiking, dancing, or golfing.
- Seek support from an ex-smoker or a supportive friend.
- Think of yourself as a nonsmoker: "I NO LONGER SMOKE."
- Avoid settings associated with smoking for the first few weeks.

- Drink plenty of water to flush nicotine from your system. Limit alcohol.
- Keep low-calorie snacks, like cucumbers or celery, handy to combat munching urges.

Your Success Starts Today: Commit to the Process

Breaking free from smoking requires consistency, commitment, and the right tools. The *Stomp on Smoking* audio recording is designed to guide your subconscious mind toward freedom and empowerment—yet it's up to you to make it a daily practice.

For best results, listen to the recording every night before bed. This is the time when your subconscious is most receptive to positive change. Let the calming, empowering suggestions take root as you relax into the process.

Remember: Your success depends on showing up for yourself each day. Make this part of your nightly routine, and watch as your cravings fade, your confidence grows, and you step into a healthier, smoke-free life. Take action now—visit healwithin.com/shop to download the recording and begin your journey today.

You deserve this transformation—start today!

IT'S OKAY TO RESTART

If you've picked up smoking again, stop negative self-talk and self-punishment—it's part of the process. Change takes time, and your subconscious mind needs consistent effort to rewrite old programming.

Every step forward counts, even if you stumble. You can stop and restart as many times as it takes. Listening to the *Stop Smoking* audio recording every night will reinforce your progress, but for deeper, lasting results, consider scheduling a one-on-one hypnosis session with me.

Together, we'll uncover and reprogram the deeper patterns keeping you stuck. Relax and let it happen! Contact me today for a consultation and let's create your smoke-free future.

🌐 **www.healwithin.com**

You've got the power to make this change—and I'm here to guide you.

AFFIRMATIONS

From this day forward...

- No activity in my life goes better with smoking.
- Every day, in every way, I am becoming more in control of my life and how I live my life
- No situation in my life requires shallow breathing.
- Everything in my life goes better with lungs full of fresh air and easy breath.
- I now surround myself with positive, proactive, loving, and appreciative people.
- I trust and have confidence in myself.
- I take full responsibility for my health.
- I remain calm and at peace as a nonsmoker
- I accomplish my mental, physical, and emotional goals each day at a time.
- Everything in my life goes better with good health.
- I remain tranquil and feel my pride grow within me.
- I treat everyone I meet with respect, sincerity, mercy, and tolerance, and expect to be respected and treated equally. Because – I Matter
- *I now Evoke what was – Embrace what is – Evolve to what will be. I Matter*

BONUS: SELF-HYPNOSIS PRACTICE FOR DEEPER HEALING

Instructions for Self-Hypnosis Practice

All hypnosis is self-hypnosis.
You may read and record this script slowly in your own voice and listen before sleep.
When your own voice speaks with calm and intention, it becomes ten times more nurturing and impactful.
Your subconscious receives it as truth — especially during quiet moments of rest.

After you record it:
Find a quiet, comfortable space where you will not be disturbed.
Sit or recline in a way that feels fully supported.
When ready, gently close your eyes and begin listening to your recording.

Self-Hypnosis: Breathe in Freedom

Now that I feel calm and supported...
I connect with my breath, my power, and my choice.
With each breath, I bring in oxygen and vitality.
With each exhale, I release all negativities.

I no longer need to suppress my emotions or seek relief outside myself.
I choose comfort, calm, and clarity within me.

I inhale strength.
I exhale the urge.
I breathe in life.
I release the dark past.

I acknowledge that this habit once served a purpose—
And I now choose a healthier, more powerful way to care for myself.

I trust that my lungs are healing.
My body is restoring.
My mind is resetting with every breath I take.

I am free.
I am clear.
I am in control.

Each day, I choose peace over craving.
Each breath I take reminds me of my freedom.

The more I return to this calm space,
The easier it becomes to say yes to life and no to old patterns.

I see myself smiling, relieved, healthier, energized.
I feel my heart thanking me.
I feel my future thanking me.

This is not about deprivation.
This is my liberation.

When I am ready, I take a deep breath in…
I bring gentle movement back to my body…
And I return to full awareness—calm, clear, and proud of my choice.

ABOUT LIZA

Why the Boubari 3E Method Works

As a Clinical Hypnotherapist, Liza Boubari is one of the most reputable smoking cessation specialists in the Greater Los Angeles area. With over two decades of experience, Liza has helped countless individuals heal within and transform their lives.

Liza says: **"I get it. I used to smoke over a pack a day."** Her journey to becoming a nonsmoker fuels her passion for helping others reclaim their health and freedom. With her Stomp on Smoking method, Liza combines hypnosis, behavioral insights, and empowering affirmations to create a proven system for success.

Liza considers it a professional honor to help others free themselves from smoking. Her personal experiences also extend to using the science of self-hypnosis for medical procedures without anesthetics, showcasing the transformative power of the mind.

Thousands of former clients attest to the power of The Boubari 3E Method, from one-pack-a-day smokers to secret smokers, social smokers, and emotional smokers. Teens, pregnant women, CEOs, veterans, doctors, teachers, and even other therapists have found success with this method.

The scope of Liza's practice includes Traditional and Ericksonian Therapy, Gestalt Therapy, Time-Line Therapy, Guided Imagery, and NLP (Neuro-Linguistic Programming). Her approach helps peel back emotional layers and uncover the freedom to embrace your true, radiant self.

Client Testimonials:

- "Not only is this book useful and informative, but it's also a no-nonsense method of breaking the habit of smoking, based on sound and refreshing reality." – Greg Krikorian, Business Life Magazine.

- "Liza isn't just an expert hypnotherapist. She integrates her work with skill and passion. I didn't just 'stop smoking' with Liza; I reclaimed my health and me... realizing that I matter." – Bob Summers.

- "In October 2001, I attended your stop-smoking class, and after 40 years, I am still a nonsmoker! My heartfelt thanks to you for a healthier me." – Nancy LaVelle, Glendale.

TAKE THE NEXT STEP

The work you have done is a testament to your courage and commitment. Trust that you are exactly where you need to be, guided by a higher energy that has always been within you. Take the first step toward healing within—you're worth it.

Book your session today. I encourage you to get the ***Stop Smoking*** self-hypnosis audio to reinforce your journey. Visit **HealWithin.com** for resources, tools, and more inspirational success stories.

Our Mission:
To empower individuals to heal within by uncovering and transforming layers of hurt and pain buried deep in the unconscious mind. **Evoke - Embrace - Evolve – You Matter.**

If you or someone you know is ready for one-on-one sessions to Stomp on Smoking, call for a free, no-obligation consultation.

Contact Us:
 818-551-1501
 www.lizabobuari.com
 www.healwithin.com

www.ingramcontent.com/pod-product-compliance
Lightning Source LLC
Chambersburg PA
CBHW050226100526
44585CB00017BA/2094